'We must learn to love, learn to be kind, and this from earliest youth . . . Likewise, hatred must be learned and nurtured, if one wishes to become a proficient hater.'

FRIEDRICH NIETZSCHE
Born 1844, Röcken, Germany
Died 1900, Weimar, Germany

Selection taken from *Human, All Too Human*,
first published in 1878.

NIETZSCHE IN PENGUIN CLASSICS
A Nietzsche Reader
Beyond Good and Evil
Ecce Homo
Human, All Too Human
On the Genealogy of Morals
The Birth of Tragedy
The Portable Nietzsche
Thus Spoke Zarathustra
Twilight of Idols and *Anti-Christ*

FRIEDRICH NIETZSCHE

Aphorisms on Love and Hate

Translated by
Marion Faber and Stephen Lehmann

PENGUIN BOOKS

PENGUIN CLASSICS

UK | USA | Canada | Ireland | Australia
India | New Zealand | South Africa

Penguin Books is part of the Penguin Random House group of companies
whose addresses can be found at global.penguinrandomhouse.com.

This selection published in Penguin Classics 2015
003

Translation copyright © Marion Faber, 1984

The moral right of the translator has been asserted

Set in 9.5/13 pt Baskerville 10 Pro
Typeset by Jouve (UK), Milton Keynes
Printed in Great Britain by Clays Ltd, St Ives plc

A CIP catalogue record for this book is available from the British Library

ISBN: 978-0-141-39790-0

www.greenpenguin.co.uk

Penguin Random House is committed to a
sustainable future for our business, our readers
and our planet. This book is made from Forest
Stewardship Council® certified paper.

The advantages of psychological observation. That meditating on things human, all too human (or, as the learned phrase goes, 'psychological observation') is one of the means by which man can ease life's burden; that by exercising this art, one can secure presence of mind in difficult situations and entertainment amid boring surroundings; indeed, that from the thorniest and unhappiest phases of one's own life one can pluck maxims and feel a bit better thereby: this was believed, known – in earlier centuries. Why has it been forgotten in this century, when many signs point, in Germany at least, if not throughout Europe, to the dearth of psychological observation? Not particularly in novels, short stories, and philosophical meditations, for these are the work of exceptional men; but more in the judging of public events and personalities; most of all we lack the art of psychological dissection and calculation in all classes of society, where one hears a lot of talk about men, but none at all *about man*. Why do people let the richest and most harmless source of entertainment get away from them? Why do they not even read the great masters of the psychological maxim any more? For it is no exaggeration to say that it is hard to find the cultured European who has read La Rochefoucauld and his spiritual and artistic cousins. Even more uncommon is the man who knows them and does not despise them. But even this unusual reader will probably find much less delight in those artists than their form ought to give him; for not even the finest mind is capable of adequate appreciation of the art of the polished maxim if he has not been educated to it, has not been challenged by it himself. Without such practical learning one takes this form of creating and forming to be easier than it is; one is not acute enough in discerning what is successful and attractive. For that reason present-day readers of maxims take a relatively insignificant delight in them, scarcely a mouthful of pleasure; they react like typical viewers of cameos, praising them because they cannot love them, and quick to admire but even quicker to run away.

*

Objection. Or might there be a counterargument to the thesis that psychological observation is one of life's best stimulants, remedies, and palliatives? Might one be so persuaded of the unpleasant consequences of this art as to intentionally divert the student's gaze from it? Indeed, a certain blind faith in the goodness of human nature, an inculcated aversion to dissecting human behavior, a kind of shame with respect to the naked soul, may really be more desirable for a man's overall happiness than the trait of psychological sharpsightedness, which is helpful in isolated instances. And perhaps the belief in goodness, in virtuous men and actions, in an abundance of impersonal goodwill in the world has made men better, in that it has made them less distrustful. If one imitates Plutarch's heroes with enthusiasm and feels an aversion toward tracing skeptically the motives for their actions, then the welfare of human society has benefited (even if the truth of human society has not). Psychological error, and dullness in this area generally, help humanity forward; but knowledge of the truth might gain more from the stimulating power of an hypothesis like the one La Rochefoucauld places at the beginning of the first edition of his *Sentences et maximes morales:* 'Ce que le monde nomme vertu n'est d'ordinaire qu'un fantôme formé par nos passions, à qui on donne un nom honnête pour faire impunément ce qu'on veut.'* La Rochefoucauld and those other French masters of soul searching (whose company a German, the author of *Psychological Observations*, has recently joined) are like accurately aimed arrows, which hit the mark again and again, the black mark of man's nature. Their skill inspires amazement, but the spectator

---

*   'That which men call virtue is usually no more than a phantom formed by our passions, to which one gives an honest name in order to do with impunity whatever one wishes.'

who is guided not by the scientific spirit, but by the humane spirit, will eventually curse an art which seems to implant in the souls of men a predilection for belittling and doubt.

*

Nevertheless. However the argument and counterargument stand, the present condition of one certain, single science has made necessary the awakening of moral observation, and mankind cannot be spared the horrible sight of the psychological operating table, with its knives and forceps. For now that science rules which asks after the origin and history of moral feelings and which tries as it progresses to pose and solve the complicated sociological problems; the old philosophy doesn't even acknowledge such problems and has always used meager excuses to avoid investigating the origin and history of moral feelings. We can survey the consequences very clearly, many examples having proven how the errors of the greatest philosophers usually start from a false explanation of certain human actions and feelings, how an erroneous analysis of so-called selfless behavior, for example, can be the basis for false ethics, for whose sake religion and mythological confusion are then drawn in, and finally how the shadows of these sad spirits also fall upon physics and the entire contemplation of the world. But if it is a fact that the superficiality of psychological observation has laid the most dangerous traps for human judgment and conclusions, and continues to lay them anew, then what we need now is a persistence in work that does not tire of piling stone upon stone, pebble upon pebble; we need a sober courage to do such humble work without shame and to defy any who disdain it. It is true that countless individual remarks about things human and all too human were first detected and stated in those social circles which would make every sort of sacrifice not for scientific knowledge, but for a witty coquetry. And because the scent of that old homeland (a very seductive scent) has attached itself almost inextricably to the whole genre of the moral maxim, the scientific man instinctively shows some suspicion towards this genre and its seriousness. But it suffices to point to the outcome: already it is becoming clear that the most serious results grow up from the ground of psychological observation. Which principle did one of the keenest and coolest thinkers, the author of the book *On the Origin of Moral Feelings*, arrive at through his incisive and piercing analysis of human actions? 'The moral man,' he says, 'stands no nearer to the intelligible (metaphysical) world than does the physical man.' Perhaps at some point in the future this principle, grown hard and sharp by the hammerblow of historical knowledge, can serve as the axe laid to the root of men's 'metaphysical need' (whether *more* as a blessing than as a curse for the general welfare, who can say?). In any event, it is a tenet with the most weighty consequences, fruitful and frightful at the same time, and seeing into the world with that double vision which all great insights have.

*

Morality and the ordering of the good. The accepted hierarchy of the good, based on how a low, higher, or a most high egoism desires that thing or the other, decides today about morality or immorality. To prefer a low good (sensual pleasure, for example) to one esteemed higher (health, for example) is taken for immoral, likewise to prefer comfort to freedom. The hierarchy of the good, however, is not fixed and identical at all times. If someone prefers revenge to justice, he is moral by the standard of an earlier culture, yet by the standard of the present culture he is immoral. 'Immoral' then indicates that someone has not felt, or not felt strongly enough, the higher, finer, more spiritual motives which the new culture of the time has brought with it. It indicates a backward nature, but only in degree.

The hierarchy itself is not established or changed from the point of view of morality; nevertheless an action is judged moral or immoral according to the prevailing determination.

*

Cruel men as backward. We must think of men who are cruel today as stages of *earlier cultures*, which have been left over; in their case, the mountain range of humanity shows openly its deeper formations, which otherwise lie hidden. They are backward men whose brains, because of various possible accidents of heredity, have not yet developed much delicacy or versatility. They show us what we *all* were, and frighten us. But they themselves are as little responsible as a piece of granite for being granite. In our brain, too, there must be grooves and bends which correspond to that state of mind, just as there are said to be reminders of the fish state in the form of certain human organs. But these grooves and bends are no longer the bed in which the river of our feeling courses.

*

Gratitude and revenge. The powerful man feels gratitude for the following reason: through his good deed, his benefactor has, as it were, violated the powerful man's sphere and penetrated it. Now through his act of gratitude the powerful man requites himself by violating the sphere of the benefactor. It is a milder form of revenge. Without the satisfaction of gratitude, the powerful man would have shown himself to be unpowerful and henceforth would be considered such. For that reason, every society of good men (that is, originally, of powerful men) places gratitude among its first duties.

Swift remarked that men are grateful in the same proportion as they cherish revenge.

*

Double prehistory of good and evil. The concept of good and evil has a double prehistory: namely, first of all, in the soul of the ruling clans and castes. The man who has the power to requite goodness with goodness, evil with evil, and really does practice requital by being grateful and vengeful, is called 'good'. The man who is unpowerful and cannot requite is taken for bad. As a good man, one belongs to the 'good', a community that has a communal feeling, because all the individuals are entwined together by their feeling for requital. As a bad man, one belongs to the 'bad', to a mass of abject, powerless men who have no communal feeling. The good men are a caste; the bad men are a multitude, like particles of dust. Good and bad are for a time equivalent to noble and base, master and slave. Conversely, one does not regard the enemy as evil: he can requite. In Homer, both the Trojan and the Greek are good. Not the man who inflicts harm on us, but the man who is contemptible, is bad. In the community of the good, goodness is hereditary; it is impossible for a bad man to grow out of such good soil. Should one of the good men nevertheless do something unworthy of good men, one resorts to excuses; one blames God, for example, saying that he struck the good man with blindness and madness.

Then, in the souls of oppressed, powerless men, every *other* man is taken for hostile, inconsiderate, exploitative, cruel, sly, whether he be noble or base. Evil is their epithet for man, indeed for every possible living being, even, for example, for a god; 'human', 'divine' mean the same as 'devilish', 'evil'. Signs of goodness, helpfulness, pity are taken anxiously for malice, the prelude to a terrible outcome, bewilderment, and deception, in short, for refined evil. With such a state of mind in the individual, a community can scarcely come about at all – or at most in the crudest form; so that wherever this concept of good and evil predominates, the downfall of individuals, their clans and races, is near at hand.

Our present morality has grown up on the ground of the *ruling* clans and castes.

*

Pity more intense than suffering. There are cases where pity is more intense than actual suffering. When one of our friends is guilty of something ignominious, for example, we feel it more painfully than when we ourselves do it. For we believe in the purity of his character more than he does. Thus our love for him (probably because of this very belief) is more intense than his own love for himself. Even if his egoism suffers more than our egoism, in that he has to feel the bad consequences of his fault more intensely, our selflessness (this word must never be taken literally, but only as a euphemism) is touched more intensely by his guilt than is his selflessness.

*

Economy of kindness. Kindness and love, the most curative herbs and agents in human intercourse, are such precious finds that one would hope these balsamlike remedies would be used as economically as possible; but this is impossible. Only the boldest Utopians would dream of the economy of kindness.

*

Goodwill. Among the small but endlessly abundant and therefore very effective things that science ought to heed more than the great, rare things, is goodwill. I mean those expressions of a friendly disposition in interactions, that smile of the eye, those handclasps, that ease which usually envelops nearly all human actions. Every teacher, every official brings this ingredient to what he considers his duty. It is the continual manifestation of our humanity, its rays of light, so to speak, in which everything grows. Especially within the narrowest circle, in the family, life sprouts and blossoms only by this goodwill. Good nature, friendliness, and courtesy of the heart are ever-flowing tributaries of the selfless drive and have made much greater contributions to culture than those much more famous expressions of this drive, called pity, charity, and self-sacrifice. But we tend to underestimate them, and in fact there really is not much about them that is selfless. The *sum* of these small doses is nevertheless mighty; its cumulative force is among the strongest of forces.

Similarly, there is much more happiness to be found in the world than dim eyes can see, if one calculates correctly and does not forget all those moments of ease which are so plentiful in every day of every human life, even the most oppressed.

*

Desire to arouse pity. In the most noteworthy passage of his self-portrait (first published in 1658), La Rochefoucauld certainly hits the mark when he warns all reasonable men against pity, when he advises them to leave it to those common people who need passions (because they are not directed by reason) to bring them to the point of helping the sufferer and intervening energetically in a misfortune. For pity, in his (and Plato's) judgment, weakens the soul. Of course one ought to *express* pity, but one ought to guard against *having* it; for unfortunate people are so *stupid* that they count the expression of pity as the greatest good on earth.

Perhaps one can warn even more strongly against having pity for the unfortunate if one does not think of their need for pity as stupidity and intellectual deficiency, a kind of mental disorder resulting from their misfortune (this is how La Rochefoucauld seems to regard it), but rather as something quite different and more dubious. Observe how children weep and cry, *so that* they will be pitied, how they wait for the moment when their condition will be noticed. Or live among the ill and depressed, and question whether their eloquent laments and whimpering, the spectacle of their misfortune, is not basically aimed at *hurting* those present. The pity that the spectators then express consoles the weak and suffering, inasmuch as they see that, despite all their weakness, they still *have* at least one *power: the power to hurt*. When expressions of pity make the unfortunate man aware of this feeling of superiority, he gets a kind of pleasure from it; his self-image revives; he is still important enough to inflict pain on the world. Thus the thirst for pity is a thirst for self-enjoyment, and at the expense of one's fellow men. It reveals man in the complete inconsideration of his most intimate dear self, but not precisely in his 'stupidity,' as La Rochefoucauld thinks.

In social dialogue, three-quarters of all questions and answers are framed in order to hurt the participants a little bit; this is why many men thirst after society so much: it gives them a feeling of their strength. In these countless, but very small doses, malevolence takes effect as one of life's powerful stimulants, just as goodwill, dispensed in the same way throughout the human world, is the perennially ready cure.

But will there be many people honest enough to admit that it is a pleasure to inflict pain? That not infrequently one amuses himself (and well) by offending other men (at least in his thoughts) and by shooting pellets of petty malice at them? Most people are too dishonest, and a few men are too good, to know anything about this source of shame. So they may try to deny that Prosper Merimée is right when he says, 'Sachez aussi qu'il n'y a rien de plus commun que de faire le mal pour le plaisir de le faire.'*

*

How seeming becomes being. Ultimately, not even the deepest pain can keep the actor from thinking of the impression of his part and the overall theatrical effect, not even, for example, at his child's funeral. He will be his own audience, and cry about his own pain as he expresses it. The hypocrite who always plays one and the same role finally ceases to be a hypocrite. Priests, for example, who are usually conscious or unconscious hypocrites when they are young men, finally end by becoming natural, and then they really are priests, with no affectation. Or if the father does not get that far, perhaps the son, using his father's headway, inherits the habit. If someone wants to *seem* to be something, stubbornly and for a long time, he

---

* 'Know that nothing is more common than to do harm for the pleasure of doing it.'

13

eventually finds it hard to *be* anything else. The profession of almost every man, even the artist, begins with hypocrisy, as he imitates from the outside, copies what is effective. The man who always wears the mask of a friendly countenance eventually has to gain power over benevolent moods without which the expression of friendliness cannot be forced – and eventually then these moods gain power over him, and he *is* benevolent.

*

Triumph of knowledge over radical evil. The man who wants to gain wisdom profits greatly from having thought for a time that man is basically evil and degenerate: this idea is wrong, like its opposite, but for whole periods of time it was predominant and its roots have sunk deep into us and into our world. To understand ourselves we must understand *it;* but to climb higher, we must then climb over and beyond it. We recognize that there are no sins in the metaphysical sense; but, in the same sense, neither are there any virtues; we recognize that this entire realm of moral ideas is in a continual state of fluctuation, that there are higher and deeper concepts of good and evil, moral and immoral. A man who desires no more from things than to understand them easily makes peace with his soul and will err (or 'sin', as the world calls it) at the most out of ignorance, but hardly out of desire. He will no longer want to condemn and root out his desires; but his single goal, governing him completely, to *understand* as well as he can at all times, will cool him down and soften all the wildness in his disposition. In addition, he has rid himself of a number of tormenting ideas; he no longer feels anything at the words 'pains of hell', 'sinfulness', 'incapacity for the good': for him they are only the evanescent silhouettes of erroneous thoughts about life and the world.

*

Morality as man's dividing himself. A good author, who really cares about his subject, wishes that someone would come and destroy him by representing the same subject more clearly and by answering every last question contained in it. The girl in love wishes that she might prove the devoted faithfulness of her love through her lover's faithlessness. The soldier wishes that he might fall on the battlefield for his victorious fatherland, for in the victory of his fatherland his greatest desire is also victorious. The mother gives the child what she takes from herself: sleep, the best food, in some instances even her health, her wealth.

Are all these really selfless states, however? Are these acts of morality *miracles* because they are, to use Schopenhauer's phrase, 'impossible and yet real'? Isn't it clear that, in all these cases, man is loving *something of himself*, a thought, a longing, an offspring, more than *something else of himself;* that he is thus *dividing up* his being and sacrificing one part for the other? Is it something *essentially* different when a pigheaded man says, 'I would rather be shot at once than move an inch to get out of that man's way'?

The *inclination towards something* (a wish, a drive, a longing) is present in all the above-mentioned cases; to yield to it, with all its consequences, is in any case not 'selfless'. In morality, man treats himself not as an 'individuum', but as a 'dividuum'.

*

What one can promise. One can promise actions, but not feelings, for the latter are involuntary. He who promises to love forever or hate forever or be forever faithful to someone is promising something that is not in his power. He can, however, promise those actions that are usually the consequence of love, hatred, or faithfulness, but that can also spring from other motives: for there are several paths and motives to an action. A promise to love someone forever, then, means, 'As long as I love you I will render unto you the actions of love; if I no longer love you, you will continue to receive the same actions from me, if for other motives.' Thus the illusion remains in the minds of one's fellow men that the love is unchanged and still the same.

One is promising that the semblance of love will

endure, then, when without self-deception one vows everlasting love.

*

Intellect and morality. One must have a good memory to be able to keep the promises one has given. One must have strong powers of imagination to be able to have pity. So closely is morality bound to the quality of the intellect.

*

Desire to avenge and vengeance. To have thoughts of revenge and execute them means to be struck with a violent – but temporary – fever. But to have thoughts of revenge without the strength or courage to execute them means to endure a chronic suffering, a poisoning of body and soul. A morality that notes only the intentions assesses both cases equally; usually the first case is assessed as worse (because of the evil consequences that the act of revenge may produce). Both evaluations are short-sighted.

*

The ability to wait. Being able to wait is so hard that the greatest poets did not disdain to make the inability to wait the theme of their poetry. Thus Shakespeare in his

Othello, Sophocles in his Ajax, who, as the oracle suggests, might not have thought his suicide necessary, if only he had been able to let his feeling cool for one day more. He probably would have outfoxed the terrible promptings of his wounded vanity and said to himself: 'Who, in my situation, has never once taken a sheep for a warrior? Is that so monstrous? On the contrary, it is something universally human.' Ajax might have consoled himself thus.

Passion will not wait. The tragedy in the lives of great men often lies not in their conflict with the times and the baseness of their fellow men, but rather in their inability to postpone their work for a year or two. They cannot wait.

In every duel, the advising friends have to determine whether the parties involved might be able to wait a while longer. If they cannot, then a duel is reasonable, since each of the parties says to himself: 'Either I continue to live, and the other must die at once, or vice versa.' In that case, to wait would be to continue suffering the horrible torture of offended honor in the presence of the offender. And this can be more suffering than life is worth.

*

Reveling in revenge. Crude men who feel themselves insulted tend to assess the degree of insult as high as possible, and talk about the offense in greatly exaggerated language, only so they can revel to their heart's content in the aroused feelings of hatred and revenge.

*

Those who flare up. We must beware of the man who flares up at us as of someone who has once made an attempt upon our life. For *that* we are still alive is due to his lacking the power to kill. If looks could kill, we would long ago have been done for. It is an act of primitive culture to bring someone to silence by making physical savageness visible, by inciting fear.

In the same way, the cold glance which elegant people use with their servants is a vestige from those castelike distinctions between man and man, an act of primitive antiquity. Women, the guardians of that which is old, have also been more faithful in preserving this cultural remnant.

*

Love and justice. Why do we overestimate love to the disadvantage of justice, saying the nicest things about it, as if it were a far higher essence than justice? Isn't love obviously more foolish? Of course, but for just that reason so much more pleasant for everyone. Love is foolish, and possesses a rich horn of plenty; from it she dispenses her gifts to everyone, even if he does not deserve them, indeed, even if he does not thank her for them. She is as nonpartisan as rain, which (according to the Bible and to experience) rains not only upon the unjust, but sometimes soaks the just man to the skin, too.

*

Degree of moral inflammability unknown. Whether or not our passions reach the point of red heat and guide our whole life depends on whether or not we have been exposed to certain shocking sights or impressions – for example a father falsely executed, killed or tortured; an unfaithful wife; a cruel ambush by an enemy. No one knows how far circumstances, pity, or indignation may drive him; he does not know the degree of his inflammability. Miserable, mean conditions make one miserable; it is usually not the quality of the experiences but rather the quantity that determines the lower and the higher man, in good and in evil.

*

The honor of the person applied to the cause. We universally honor acts of love and sacrifice for the sake of one's neighbor, wherever we find them. In this way we heighten the *value of the things* loved in that way, or for which sacrifices are made, even though they are in themselves perhaps not worth much. A valiant army convinces us about the cause for which it is fighting.

*

Misunderstanding between the sufferer and the perpetrator. When a rich man takes a possession from a poor man (for example, when a prince robs a plebeian of his sweetheart), the poor man misunderstands. He thinks that the rich man must be a villain to take from him the little he has. But the rich man does not feel the value of a *particular* possession so deeply because he is accustomed to having many. So he cannot put himself in the place of the poor man, and he is by no means doing as great an injustice as the poor man believes. Each has a false idea of the other. The injustice of the mighty, which enrages us most in history, is by no means as great as it appears. Simply the inherited feeling of being a higher being, with higher pretensions, makes one rather cold, and leaves the conscience at peace. Indeed, none of us feels anything like injustice when there is a great difference between ourselves and some other being, and we kill a gnat, for example, without any twinge of conscience. So it is no sign of wickedness in Xerxes (whom even all the Greeks portray as exceptionally noble) when he takes a son from his father and has him cut to pieces, because the father had expressed an anxious and doubtful distrust of their entire campaign. In this case the individual man is eliminated like an unpleasant insect; he stands too low to be allowed to keep on arousing bothersome feelings in a world ruler. Indeed, no cruel man is cruel to the extent that the mistreated man believes. The idea of pain is not the same as the suffering of it. It is the same with an unjust judge, with a journalist who misleads public opinion by little dishonesties. In each of these cases, cause and effect are experienced in quite different categories of thought and feeling; nevertheless, it is automatically assumed that the perpetrator and sufferer think and feel the same, and the guilt of the one is therefore measured by the pain of the other.

*

Malice is rare. Most men are much too concerned with themselves to be malicious.

*

Limit of human love. Any man who has once declared the other man to be a fool, a bad fellow, is annoyed when that man ends by showing that he is not.

*

Mores and morality. To be moral, correct, ethical means to obey an age-old law or tradition. Whether one submits to it gladly or with difficulty makes no difference; enough that one submits. We call 'good' the man who does the moral thing as if by nature, after a long history of inheritance – that is, easily, and gladly, whatever it is (he will, for example, practice revenge when that is considered moral, as in the older Greek culture). He is called good because he is good 'for' something. But because, as mores changed, goodwill, pity, and the like were always felt to be 'good for' something, useful, it is primarily the man of goodwill, the helpful man, who is called 'good'. To be evil is to be 'not moral' (immoral), to practice bad habits, go against tradition, however reasonable or stupid it may be. To harm one's fellow, however, has been felt primarily as injurious in all moral codes of different times, so that when we hear the word 'bad' now, we think particularly of voluntary injury to one's fellow. When men determine between moral and immoral, good and evil, the basic opposition is not 'egoism' and 'selflessness', but rather adherence to a tradition or law, and release from it. The *origin* of the tradition makes no difference, at least concerning good and evil, or an immanent categorical imperative; but is rather above all for the purpose of maintaining *a community*, a people. Every superstitious custom, originating in a coincidence that is interpreted falsely, forces a tradition that it is moral to follow. To release oneself from it is dangerous, even more injurious for the *community* than for the individual (because the divinity punishes the whole community for sacrilege and violation of its rights, and the individual only as a part of that community). Now, each tradition grows more venerable the farther its origin lies in the past, the more it is forgotten; the respect paid to the tradition accumulates from generation to generation; finally the origin becomes sacred and awakens awe; and thus the morality of piety is in any case much older than that morality which requires selfless acts.

*

Pleasure in custom. An important type of pleasure, and thus an important source of morality, grows out of habit. One does habitual things more easily, skillfully, gladly; one feels a pleasure at them, knowing from experience that the habit has stood the test and is useful. A morality one can live with has been proved salutary, effective, in contrast to all the as yet unproven new experiments. Accordingly, custom is the union of the pleasant and the useful; in addition, it requires no thought. As soon as man can exercise force, he exercises it to introduce and enforce his mores, for to him they represent proven wisdom. Likewise, a community will force each individual in it to the same mores. Here is the error: because one feels good with one custom, or at least because he lives his life by means of it, this custom is necessary, for he holds it to be the *only* possibility by which one can feel good; the enjoyment of life seems to grow out of it alone.

This idea of habit as a condition of existence is carried right into the smallest details of custom: since lower peoples and cultures have only very slight insight into the real causality, they make sure, with superstitious fear, that everything take the same course; even where a custom is difficult, harsh, burdensome, it is preserved because it seems to be highly useful. They do not know that the same degree of comfort can also exist with other customs and that even higher degrees of comfort can be attained. But they do perceive that all customs, even the harshest, become more pleasant and mild with time, and that even the severest way of life can become a habit and thus a pleasure.

*

Pleasure and social instinct. From his relationship to other men, man gains a new kind of pleasure, in addition to those pleasurable feelings which he gets from himself. In this way he widens significantly the scope of his pleasurable feelings. Perhaps some of these feelings have come down to him from the animals, who visibly feel pleasure when playing with each other, particularly mothers playing with their young. Next one might think of sexual relations, which make virtually every lass seem interesting to every lad (and vice versa) in view of potential pleasure. Pleasurable feeling based on human relations generally makes man better; shared joy, pleasure taken together, heightens this feeling; it gives the individual security, makes him better-natured, dissolves distrust and envy: one feels good oneself and can see the other man feel good in the same way. *Analogous expressions of pleasure* awaken the fantasy of empathy, the feeling of being alike. Shared sorrows do it, too: the same storms, dangers, enemies. Upon this basis man has built the oldest covenant, whose purpose is to eliminate and resist communally any threatening unpleasure, for the good of each individual. And thus social instinct grows out of pleasure.

*

Innocence of so-called evil actions. All 'evil' actions are motivated by the drive for preservation, or, more exactly, by the individual's intention to gain pleasure and avoid unpleasure; thus they are motivated, but they are not evil. 'Giving pain in and of itself' *does not exist*, except in the brain of philosophers, nor does 'giving pleasure in and of itself' (pity, in the Schopenhauerian sense). In conditions *preceding* organized states, we kill any being, be it ape or man, that wants to take a fruit off a tree before we do, just when we are hungry and running up to the tree. We would treat the animal the same way today, if we were hiking through inhospitable territory.

Those evil actions which outrage us most today are based on the error that that man who harms us has free will, that is, that he had the *choice* not to do this bad thing to us. This belief in his choice arouses hatred, thirst for revenge, spite, the whole deterioration of our imagination; whereas we get much less angry at an animal because we consider it irresponsible. To do harm not out of a drive for preservation, but for requital – that is the result of an erroneous judgment, and is therefore likewise innocent. The individual can, in conditions preceding the organized state, treat others harshly and cruelly to *intimidate* them, to secure his existence through such intimidating demonstrations of his power. This is how the brutal, powerful man acts, the original founder of a state, who subjects to himself those who are weaker. He has the right to do it, just as the state now takes the right. Or rather, there is no right that can prevent it. The ground for all morality can only be prepared when a greater individual or collective-individual, as, for example, society or the state, subjects the individuals in it, that is, when it draws them out of their isolatedness and integrates them into a union. *Force* precedes morality; indeed, for a time morality itself is force, to which others acquiesce to avoid unpleasure. Later it becomes custom, and still later free obedience, and finally almost instinct: then it is coupled to pleasure, like all habitual and natural things, and is now called *virtue*.

*

Judge not. When we consider earlier periods, we must be careful not to fall into unjust abuse. The injustice of slavery, the cruelty in subjugating persons and peoples, cannot be measured by our standards. For the instinct for justice was not so widely developed then. Who has the right to reproach Calvin of Geneva for burning Dr Servet? His was a consistent act, flowing out of his convictions, and the Inquisition likewise had its reasons; it is just that the views dominant then were wrong and resulted in a consistency that we find harsh, because we now find those views so alien. Besides, what is the burning of one man compared to the eternal pains of hell for nearly everyone! And yet this much more terrible idea used to dominate the whole world without doing any essential damage to the idea of a god. In our own time, we treat political heretics harshly and cruelly, but because we have learned to believe in the necessity of the state we are not as sensitive to this cruelty as we are to that cruelty whose justification we reject. Cruelty to animals, by children and Italians, stems from ignorance; namely, in the interests of its teachings, the church has placed the animal too far beneath man.

Likewise, in history much that is frightful and inhuman, which one would almost like not to believe, is mitigated by the observation that the commander and the executor are different people: the former does not witness his cruelty and therefore has no strong impression of it in his imagination; the latter is obeying a superior and feels no responsibility. Because of a lack of imagination, most princes and military leaders can easily appear to be harsh and cruel, without being so.

Egoism is not evil, for the idea of one's 'neighbor' (the word has a Christian origin and does not reflect the truth) is very weak in us; and we feel toward him almost as free and irresponsible as toward plants and stones. That the other suffers *must be learned;* and it can never be learned completely.

*

Harmlessness of malice. Malice does not aim at the suffering of the other in and of itself, but rather at our own enjoyment, for example, a feeling of revenge or a strong nervous excitement. Every instance of teasing shows that it gives us pleasure to release our power on the other person and experience an enjoyable feeling of superiority. Is the *immoral* thing about it, then, to have *pleasure on the basis of other people's unpleasure?* Is *Schadenfreude* devilish, as Schopenhauer says? Now, in nature, we take pleasure in breaking up twigs, loosening stones, fighting with wild animals, in order to gain awareness of our own strength. Is the *knowledge*, then, that another person is suffering because of us supposed to make immoral the same thing about which we otherwise feel no responsibility? But if one did not have this knowledge, one would not have that pleasure in his own superiority, which can *be discovered* only in the suffering of the other, in teasing, for example. All joy in oneself is neither good nor bad; where should the determination come from that to have pleasure in oneself one may not cause unpleasure in others? Solely from the point of view of advantage, that is, from consideration of the *consequences*, of possible unpleasure, when the injured party or the state representing him leads us to expect requital and revenge; this alone can have been the original basis for denying oneself these actions.

Pity does not aim at the pleasure of others any more than malice (as we said above) aims at the pain of others, per se. For in pity at least two (maybe many more) elements of personal pleasure are contained, and it is to that extent self-enjoyment: first of all, it is the pleasure of the emotion (the kind of pity we find in tragedy) and second, when it drives us to act, it is the pleasure of our satisfaction in the exercise of power. If, in addition, a suffering person is very close to us, we reduce our own suffering by our acts of pity.

Aside from a few philosophers, men have always placed pity rather low in the hierarchy of moral feelings – and rightly so.

*

Self-defense. If we accept self-defense as moral, then we must also accept nearly all expressions of so-called immoral egoism; we inflict harm, rob or kill, to preserve or protect ourselves, to prevent personal disaster; where cunning and dissimulation are the correct means of self-preservation, we lie. *To do injury intentionally*, when it is a matter of our existence or security (preservation of our well-being) is conceded to be moral; the state itself injures from this point of view when it imposes punishment. Of course, there can be no immorality in unintentional injury; there coincidence governs. Can there be a kind of intentional injury where it is *not* a matter of our existence, the preservation of our well-being? Can there be an injury out of pure *malice*, in cruelty, for example? If one does not know how painful an action is, it cannot be malicious; thus the child is not malicious or evil to an animal: he examines and destroys it like a toy. But do we ever completely *know* how painful an action is to the other person? As far as our nervous system extends, we protect ourselves from pain; if it extended further, right into our fellow men, we would not do harm to anyone (except in such cases where we do it to ourselves, that is, where we cut ourselves in order to cure ourselves, exert and strain ourselves to be healthy). We *conclude* by analogy that something hurts another, and through our memory and power of imagination we ourselves can feel ill at such a thought. But what difference remains between a toothache and the ache (pity) evoked by the sight of a toothache? That is, when we injure out of so-called malice, the *degree* of pain produced is in any case unknown to us; but in that we feel *pleasure* in the action (feeling of our own power, our own strong excitement) the action takes place to preserve the well-being of the individual and thus falls within a point of view similar to that of self-defence or a white lie. No life without pleasure; the struggle for pleasure is the struggle for life. Whether the individual fights this battle in ways such that men call him *good* or such that they call him *evil* is determined by the measure and makeup of his intellect.

*

Censor vitae.* For a long time, the inner state of a man who wants to become free in his judgments about life will be characterized by an alternation between love and hatred; he does not forget, and resents everything, good as well as evil. Finally, when the whole tablet of his soul is written full with experiences, he will neither despise and hate existence nor love it, but rather lie above it, now with a joyful eye, now with a sorrowful eye, and, like nature, be now of a summery, now of an autumnal disposition.

*

Secondary result. Whoever seriously wants to become free, will in the process also lose, uncoerced, the inclination

*   *Censor vitae:* critic of life.

to faults and vices; he will also be prey ever more rarely to annoyance and irritation. For his will desires nothing more urgently than knowledge, and the means to it – that is, the enduring condition in which he is best able to engage in knowledge.

*

Caution of free spirits. Free-spirited people, living for knowledge alone, will soon find they have achieved their external goal in life, their ultimate position vis à vis society and the state, and gladly be satisfied, for example, with a minor position or a fortune that just meets their needs; for they will set themselves up to live in such a way that a great change in economic conditions, even a revolution in political structures, will not overturn their life with it. They expend as little energy as possible on all these things, so that they can plunge with all their assembled energy, as if taking a deep breath, into the element of knowledge. They can then hope to dive deep, and also get a look at the bottom.

Such a spirit will be happy to take only the corner of an experience; he does not love things in the whole breadth and prolixity of their folds; for he does not want to get wrapped up in them.

He, too, knows the week-days of bondage, dependence, and service. But from time to time he must get a Sunday of freedom, or else he will not endure life.

It is probable that even his love of men will be cautious and somewhat shortwinded, for he wants to engage himself with the world of inclination and blindness only as far as is necessary for the sake of knowledge. He must trust that the genius of justice will say something on behalf of its disciple and protégé, should accusatory voices call him poor in love.

In his way of living and thinking, there is a *refined heroism;* he scorns to offer himself to mass worship, as his cruder brother does, and is used to going quietly through the world and out of the world. Whatever labyrinths he may wander through, among whatever rocks his river may at times have forced its tortured course – once he gets to the light, he goes his way brightly, lightly, and almost soundlessly, and lets the sunshine play down to his depths.

*

Lack of intimacy. Lack of intimacy among friends is a mistake that cannot be censured without becoming irreparable.

*

Twofold kind of equality. The craving for equality can be expressed either by the wish to draw all others down to one's level (by belittling, excluding, tripping them up) or by the wish to draw oneself up with everyone else (by appreciating, helping, taking pleasure in others' success).

*

Trust and intimacy If someone assiduously seeks to force intimacy with another person, he usually is not sure whether he possesses that person's trust. If someone is sure of being trusted, he places little value on intimacy.

*

Balance of friendship. Sometimes in our relationship to another person, the right balance of friendship is restored when we put a few grains of injustice on our own side of the scale.

*

Making them wait. A sure way to provoke people and to put evil thoughts into their heads is to make them wait a long time. This gives rise to immorality.

*

Means of compensation. If we have injured someone, giving him the opportunity to make a joke about us is often enough to provide him personal satisfaction, or even to win his good will.

*

Motive for attack. We attack not only to hurt a person, to conquer him, but also, perhaps, simply to become aware of our own strength.

*

The sympathetic. Sympathetic natures, always helpful in a misfortune, are rarely the same ones who share our joy: when others are happy, they have nothing to do, become superfluous, do not feel in possession of their superiority, and therefore easily show dissatisfaction.

*

Silence. For both parties, the most disagreeable way of responding to a polemic is to be angry and keep silent: for the aggressor usually takes the silence as a sign of disdain.

*

The friend's secret. There will be but few people who, when at a loss for topics of conversation, will not reveal the more secret affairs of their friends.

*

Vexation at the goodwill of others. We are wrong about the degree to which we believe ourselves hated or feared; for we ourselves know well the degree of our divergence from a person, a direction, or a party, but those others know us only very superficially, and therefore also hate us only superficially. Often we encounter goodwill which we cannot explain; but if we understand it, it offends us, for it shows that one doesn't take us seriously or importantly enough.

*

Traitor's tour-de-force. To express to your fellow conspirator the hurtful suspicion that he might be betraying you, and this at the very moment when you are yourself engaged in betraying him, is a tour-de-force of malice, because it makes the other person aware of himself and forces him to behave very unsuspiciously and openly for a time, giving you, the true traitor, a free hand.

*

To offend and be offended. It is much more agreeable to offend and later ask forgiveness than to be offended and grant forgiveness. The one who does the former demonstrates his power and then his goodness. The other, if he

37

does not want to be thought inhuman, *must* forgive; because of this coercion, pleasure in the other's humiliation is slight.

*

The talent for friendship. Among men who have a particular gift for friendship, two types stand out. The one man is in a continual state of ascent, and finds an exactly appropriate friend for each phase of his development. The series of friends that he acquires in this way is only rarely interconnected, and sometimes discordant and contradictory, quite in accordance with the fact that the later phases in his development invalidate or compromise the earlier phases. Such a man may jokingly be called a *ladder*.

The other type is represented by the man who exercises his powers of attraction on very different characters and talents, thereby winning a whole circle of friends; and these come into friendly contact with one another through him, despite all their diversity. Such a man can be called a *circle;* for in him, that intimate connection of so many different temperaments and natures must somehow be prefigured.

In many people, incidentally, the gift of having good friends is much greater than the gift of being a good friend.

*

About friends. Just think to yourself some time how different are the feelings, how divided the opinions, even among the closest acquaintances; how even the same opinions have quite a different place or intensity in the heads of your friends than in your own; how many hundreds of times there is occasion for misunderstanding or hostile flight. After all that, you will say to yourself: 'How unsure is the ground on which all our bonds and friendships rest; how near we are to cold downpours or ill weather; how lonely is every man!' If someone understands this, and also that all his fellow men's opinions, their kind and intensity, are as inevitable and irresponsible as their actions; if he learns to perceive that there is this inner inevitability of opinions, due to the indissoluble interweaving of character, occupation, talent, and environment – then he will perhaps be rid of the bitterness and sharpness of that feeling with which the wise man called out: 'Friends, there are no friends!' Rather, he will admit to himself that there are, indeed, friends, but they were brought to you by error and deception about yourself; and they must have learned to be silent in order to remain your friend; for almost always, such human relationships rest on the fact that a certain few things are never said, indeed that they are never touched upon; and once these pebbles are set rolling, the friendship follows after, and falls apart. Are there men who cannot be fatally wounded, were they to learn what their most intimate friends really know about them?

By knowing ourselves and regarding our nature itself as a changing sphere of opinions and moods, thus learning to despise it a bit, we bring ourselves into balance with others again. It is true, we have good reason to despise each of our acquaintances, even the greatest; but we have just as good reason to turn this feeling against ourselves.

And so let us bear with each other, since we do in fact bear with ourselves; and perhaps each man will some day know the more joyful hour in which he says:

'Friends, there are no friends!' the dying wise man shouted.

'Enemies, there is no enemy!' shout I, the living fool.

*

Friendship and marriage. The best friend will probably get the best wife, because a good marriage is based on a talent for friendship.

*

From the mother. Everyone carries within him an image of woman that he gets from his mother; that determines whether he will honor women in general, or despise them, or be generally indifferent to them.

*

A kind of jealousy. Mothers are easily jealous of their sons' friends if they are exceptionally successful. Usually a mother loves *herself* in her son more than she loves the son himself.

*

Different sighs. A few men have sighed because their women were abducted; most, because no one wanted to abduct them.

*

Love matches. Marriages that are made for love (so-called love matches) have Error as their father and Necessity (need) as their mother.

*

Women's friendship. Women can very well enter into a friendship with a man, but to maintain it – a little physical antipathy must help out.

*

Unity of place, and drama. If spouses did not live together, good marriages would be more frequent.

*

To want to be in love. Fiancés who have been brought together by convenience often try to *be* in love in order to overcome the reproach of cold, calculating advantage. Likewise, those who turn to Christianity for their advantage try to become truly pious, for in that way the religious pantomime is easier for them.

*

No standstill in love. A musician who *loves* the slow tempo will take the same pieces slower and slower. Thus there is no standstill in any love.

*

Proteus nature. For the sake of love, women wholly become what they are in the imagination of the men who love them.

*

Loving and possessing. Women usually love an important man in such a way that they want to have him to themselves. They would gladly put him under lock and key, if their vanity, which wants him to appear important in front of others, too, did not advise against it.

*

Masks. There are women who have no inner life wherever one looks for it, being nothing but masks. That man is to be pitied who lets himself in with such ghostly, necessarily unsatisfying creatures; but just these women are able to stimulate man's desire most intensely: he searches for their souls – and searches on and on.

*

Marriage as a long conversation. When entering a marriage, one should ask the question: do you think you will be able to have good conversations with this woman right into old age? Everything else in marriage is transitory, but most of the time in interaction is spent in conversation.

*

The female intellect. Women's intellect is manifested as perfect control, presence of mind, and utilization of all advantages. They bequeath it as their fundamental character to their children, and the father furnishes the darker background of will. His influence determines the rhythm and harmony, so to speak, to which the new life is to be played out; but its melody comes from the woman.

To say it for those who know how to explain a thing: women have the intelligence, men the heart and passion.

This is not contradicted by the fact that men actually get so much farther with their intelligence: they have the deeper, more powerful drives; these take their intelligence, which is in itself something passive, forward. Women are often privately amazed at the great honor men pay to their hearts. When men look especially for a profound, warm-hearted being, in choosing their spouse, and women for a clever, alert, and brilliant being, one sees very clearly how a man is looking for an idealized man, and a woman for an idealized woman – that is, not for a complement, but for the perfection of their own merits.

*

Short-sighted people are amorous. Sometimes just a stronger pair of glasses will cure an amorous man; and if someone had the power to imagine a face or form twenty years older, he might go through life quite undisturbed.

*

Love. The idolatry that women practice when it comes to love is fundamentally and originally a clever device, in that all those idealizations of love heighten their own power and portray them as ever more desirable in the eyes of men. But because they have grown accustomed over the centuries to this exaggerated estimation of love, it has happened that they have run into their own net and for-gotten the reason behind it. They themselves are now more deceived than men, and suffer more, therefore, from the disappointment that almost inevitably enters the life of every woman – to the extent that she even has enough fantasy and sense to be able to be deceived and disappointed.

*

Letting oneself be loved. Because one of the two loving people is usually the lover, the other the beloved, the belief has arisen that in every love affair the amount of love is constant: the more of it one of the two grabs to himself, the less remains for the other person. Sometimes, exceptionally, it happens that vanity convinces each of the two people that *he* is the one who has to be loved, so that both want to let themselves be loved: in marriage, especially, this results in some half-droll, half-absurd scenes.

*

Who suffers more? After a personal disagreement and quar-rel between a woman and a man, the one party suffers most at the thought of having hurt the other; while that other party suffers most at the thought of not having hurt the first enough; for which reason it tries by tears, sobs, and contorted features, to weigh down the other person's heart, even afterwards.

*

Opportunity for female generosity. Once a man's thoughts have gone beyond the demands of custom, he might consider whether nature and reason do not dictate that he marry several times in succession, so that first, aged twenty-two years, he marry an older girl who is spiritually and morally superior to him and can guide him through the dangers of his twenties (ambition, hatred, self-contempt, passions of all kinds). This woman's love would later be completely transformed into maternal feeling, and she would not only tolerate it, but promote it in the most salutary way, if the man in his thirties made an alliance with a quite young girl, whose education he himself would take in hand.

For one's twenties, marriage is a necessary institution; for one's thirties, it is useful, but not necessary; for later life, it often becomes harmful and promotes a husband's spiritual regression.

*

Tragedy of childhood. Not infrequently, noble-minded and ambitious men have to endure their harshest struggle in childhood, perhaps by having to assert their characters against a low-minded father, who is devoted to pretense and mendacity, or by living, like Lord Byron, in continual struggle with a childish and wrathful mother. If one has experienced such struggles, for the rest of his life he will never get over knowing who has been in reality his greatest and most dangerous enemy.

*

From the future of marriage. Those noble, free-minded women who set themselves the task of educating and elevating the female sex should not overlook one factor: marriage, conceived of in its higher interpretation, the spiritual friendship of two people of opposite sexes, that is, marriage as hoped for by the future, entered into for the purpose of begetting and raising a new generation. Such a marriage, which uses sensuality as if it were only a rare, occasional means for a higher end, probably requires and must be provided with a natural aid: *concubinage.* For if, for reasons of the man's health, his wife is also to serve for the sole satisfaction of his sexual need, a false point of view, counter to the goals we have indicated, will be decisive in choosing a wife. Posterity becomes a coincidental objective; its successful education, highly improbable. A good wife, who should be friend, helpmate, child-bearer, mother, head of the family, manager, indeed, who perhaps has to run her own business or office separate from her husband, cannot be a concubine at the same time: it would usually be asking too much of her. Thus, the opposite of what happened in Pericles' times in Athens could occur in the future: men, whose wives were not much more than concubines then, turned to Aspasias as well, because they desired the delights of a mentally and emotionally liberating sociability, which only the grace and spiritual flexibility of women can provide. All human institutions, like marriage, permit only a moderate degree of practical idealization, failing which, crude measures immediately become necessary.

*

Happiness of marriage. Everything habitual draws an ever tighter net of spiderwebs around us; then we notice that the fibres have become traps, and that we ourselves are sitting in the middle, like a spider that got caught there and must feed on its own blood. That is why the free spirit hates all habits and rules, everything enduring and definitive; that is why, again and again, he painfully tears apart the net around him, even though he will suffer as a consequence from countless large and small wounds – for he must tear those fibres *away from himself*, from his body, his soul. He must learn to love where he used to hate, and vice versa. Indeed, nothing may be impossible for him, not even to sow dragons' teeth on the same field where he previously emptied the cornucopias of his kindness.

From this one can judge whether he is cut out for the happiness of marriage.

*

Too close. If we live in too close proximity to a person, it is as if we kept touching a good etching with our bare fingers; one day we have poor, dirty paper in our hands and nothing more. A human being's soul is likewise worn down by continual touching; at least it finally *appears* that way to us – we never see its original design and beauty again.

One always loses by all-too-intimate association with women and friends; and sometimes one loses the pearl of his life in the process.

*

Voluntary sacrificial animal. Significant women bring relief to the lives of their husbands, if the latter are famous and great, by nothing so much as by becoming a vessel, so to speak, for other people's general ill-will and occasional bad humor. Contemporaries tend to overlook their great men's many mistakes and follies, even gross injustices, if only they can find someone whom they may abuse and slaughter as a veritable sacrificial animal to relieve their feelings. Not infrequently a woman finds in herself the ambition to offer herself for this sacrifice, and then the man can of course be very contented – in the case that he is egoist enough to tolerate in his vicinity such a voluntary conductor of lightning, storm, and rain.

*

Ceterum censeo.* It is ludicrous when a have-not society declares the abolition of inheritance rights, and no less ludicrous when childless people work on the practical laws of a country: they do not have enough ballast in their ship to be able to sail surely into the ocean of the future. But it seems just as nonsensical if a man who has chosen as his task the acquisition of the most general knowledge and the evaluation of the whole of existence weighs himself down with personal considerations of a family, a livelihood, security, respect of his wife and child; he is spreading out over his telescope a thick veil, which scarcely any rays from the distant heavens are able to penetrate. So I, too, come to the tenet that in questions of the highest philosophical kind, all married people are suspect.

*

Passion for things. He who directs his passion to things (the sciences, the national good, cultural interests, the arts)

*   'Incidentally, I am of the opinion.'

takes much of the fire out of his passion for people (even when they represent those things, as statesmen, philosophers, and artists represent their creations).

*

The right profession. Men seldom endure a profession if they do not believe or persuade themselves that it is basically more important than all others. Women do the same with their lovers.

*

Friend. Shared joy, not compassion, makes a friend.

*

More troublesome than enemies. When some reason (e.g., gratitude) obliges us to maintain the appearance of unqualified congeniality with people about whose own congenial behavior we are not entirely convinced, these people torment our imagination much more than do our enemies.

*

Wanting to be loved. The demand to be loved is the greatest kind of arrogance.

*

Contempt for people. The least ambiguous sign of a disdain for people is this: that one tolerates everyone else only as a means to *his* end, or not at all.

*

The life of the enemy. Whoever lives for the sake of combating an enemy has an interest in the enemy's staying alive.

*

Want of friends. A want of friends points to envy or arrogance. Many a man owes his friends simply to the fortunate circumstance that he has no cause for envy.

*

Love and hatred. Love and hatred are not blind, but are blinded by the fire they themselves carry with them.

*

Punctum saliens* of passion. He who is about to fall into a state of anger or violent love reaches a point where his

*   *the salient point*

soul is full like a vessel; but it needs one more drop of water: the good will to passion (which is generally also called the bad will). Only this little point is necessary; then the vessel runs over.

*

The hour-hand of life. Life consists of rare, isolated moments of the greatest significance, and of innumerably many intervals, during which at best the silhouettes of those moments hover about us. Love, springtime, every beautiful melody, mountains, the moon, the sea – all these speak completely to the heart but once, if in fact they ever do get a chance to speak completely. For many men do not have those moments at all, and are themselves intervals and intermissions in the symphony of real life.

*

Learning to love. We must learn to love, learn to be kind, and this from earliest youth; if education or chance give us no opportunity to practice these feelings, our soul becomes dry and unsuited even to understanding the tender inventions of loving people. Likewise, hatred must be learned and nurtured, if one wishes to become a proficient hater: otherwise the germ for that, too, will gradually wither.

*

Love and respect. Love desires; fear avoids. That is why it is impossible, at least in the same time span, to be loved and respected by the same person. For the man who respects another, acknowledges his power; that is, he fears it: his condition is one of awe. But love acknowledges no power, nothing that separates, differentiates, ranks higher or subordinates. Because the state of being loved carries with it no respect, ambitious men secretly or openly balk against it.

*

Love as a device. Whoever wants really to get to *know* something new (be it a person, an event, or a book) does well to take up this new thing with all possible love, to avert his eye quickly from, even to forget, everything about it that he finds inimical, objectionable, or false. So, for example, we give the author of a book the greatest possible head start, and, as if at a race, virtually yearn with a pounding heart for him to reach his goal. By doing this, we penetrate into the heart of the new thing, into its motive centre: and this is what it means to get to know it. Once we have got that far, reason then sets its limits; that overestimation, that occasional unhinging of the critical pendulum, was just a device to entice the soul of a matter out into the open.

*

Seriousness in play. At sunset in Genoa, I heard from a tower a long chiming of bells: it kept on and on, and over the noise of the backstreets, as if insatiable for itself, it rang out into the evening sky and the sea air, so terrible and so childish at the same time, so melancholy. Then I thought of Plato's words and felt them suddenly in my heart: *all in all, nothing human is worth taking very seriously; nevertheless . . .*